A GUIDE TO READING
SHAKESPEARE'S *A MIDSUMMER NIGHT'S DREAM*

A GUIDE TO READING SHAKESPEARE'S *A MIDSUMMER NIGHT'S DREAM*

MARIA FRANZISKA FAHEY

Maria Franziska Fahey is the author of *Metaphor and Shakespearean Drama: Unchaste Signification*, which was shortlisted for the 2012 Shakespeare's Globe Book Award. She is a member of the faculty at Friends Seminary, where she has taught English for more than twenty-five years.

Copyright © 2016 by Maria Franziska Fahey

All rights reserved.

Except for the use of brief quotations in a book review, no part of this book may be reproduced in any form by any electronic or mechanical means without the express written permission of the author.

First Printing, 2016
Second Printing, 2022, contains corrections of the text.

ISBN-13: 978-0-692-79605-4
ISBN-10: 0-692-79605-3

Accabonac Press
61 Jane Street, Suite 17C, New York, NY 10014

Cover illustration and design by Lauren Simkin Berke

for J.J.

CONTENTS

Preface ix

    On the Pleasures & Challenges of Reading Shakespeare's Dramatic Language ix

    Using This Guide xi

    Hearing & Seeing Performances xi

Questions to Consider as You Read *A Midsummer Night's Dream* 1

    Larger Questions 1

    Patterns of Figurative Language 2

    Act 1, Scene 1 3

    Act 1, Scene 2 15

    Act 2, Scene 1 19

    Act 2, Scene 2 29

    Act 3, Scene 1 35

    Act 3, Scene 2 40

    Act 4, Scene 1 53

    Act 4, Scene 2 62

    Act 5, Scene 1 64

Appendices 73

    1. Listening for Meter—An Introduction 73

    2. Reading Figurative Language—An Introduction to Metaphor, Simile, Metonymy, &

    Synecdoche 77

    3. On How an Edition of *A Midsummer Night's Dream* Is Made 85

Acknowledgments 87

PREFACE

On the Pleasures & Challenges of Reading Shakespeare's Dramatic Language

Reading Shakespeare's plays can be immensely pleasurable, but doing so is no easy task. Whereas we now get a great deal of our information through visual images, including photographs and film, in Shakespeare's day most information came through spoken language. Part of the fun, and also the challenge, of reading a Shakespeare play is having to transform language into visual images for ourselves.

Indeed, Shakespeare was aware of the demands he was making of his audiences. In the Prologue to his play *The Life of Henry the Fifth*, the Chorus admits that it cannot bring King Henry himself or "the vasty fields of France" into the theater and so asks the members of the audience to let the play work on their "imaginary forces" (*Henry V* Pro. 12, 18). The Chorus goes on to suggest, "Think, when we talk of horses, that you see them, / Printing their proud hoofs i'th' receiving earth" (Pro. 26-7).

A Shakespeare play is largely "talk"—a series of conversations among a cast of characters. However, the talk of a Shakespeare play is often more difficult to understand than ordinary speech because it has been crafted to bring a whole world before our eyes. The series of questions in this guide is designed to help you listen carefully, scene-by-scene, to what the characters say so that you can use your "imaginary forces" to see the world of *A Midsummer Night's Dream* for yourself. As you read the play's language and begin to envision its world, it will be helpful to remain aware of how the language spoken by characters in the play is different from that of ordinary speech. Here are a few of these differences:

Vocabulary. Written over 400 years ago, the plays are known for their unusually large vocabularies, including many words that were, at the time, new to the English language—some probably invented by Shakespeare himself. Almost all readers find the rich vocabulary of a Shakespeare play challenging to understand even as they come to enjoy the subtle and abundant connotations of the words Shakespeare chose. Furthermore, twenty-first century readers will find that the meanings of some words have changed since Shakespeare's day and that other words, rarely spoken now, have become obsolete. Consider, for instance, the word *sinister* in Snout's announcement: "And this the cranny is, right and sinister, / Through which the fearful lovers are to whisper" (*A Midsummer Night's Dream* 5.1.163-4). Here *sinister* means "on the left side," which is rarely how we use the word today. Or, take the word *translated* in what Quince says to Bottom after Puck magically turns Bottom's head into an ass's head: "Thou art translated" (3.1.103). Although nowadays the word *translate* usually refers to turning one language into another, in Shakespeare's day, *translation* could refer to transformation more generally.

Be sure to consult the notes in your copy of the play and to keep a good dictionary at hand, one that provides older meanings of words. (Check your library's print or online version of *The Oxford English Dictionary*—the *OED*—which is the most comprehensive English dictionary.) But don't feel obligated to look up every word when first reading a play. You can understand a great deal about unfamiliar words from their context. Consider the word *changeling* in Puck's description of Titania and Oberon's conflict:

> For Oberon is passing fell and wrath
> Because that she as her attendant hath
> A lovely boy, stol'n from an Indian king.
> She never had so sweet a changeling.
> And jealous Oberon would have the child
> Knight of his train, to trace the forests wild. (2.1.20-5)

Changeling refers to the "lovely boy" whom Puck claims Titania has stolen, "the child" whom Oberon wants for his train. Thus, a *changeling* must be a stolen child. (The *Oxford English Dictionary* defines *changeling* as "A child secretly substituted for another in infancy; *esp.* a child . . . supposed to have been left by fairies in exchange for one stolen" [*OED* 3].)

∞ Poetic Language. The conversations in a Shakespeare play are no ordinary conversations: they were crafted by a poet-playwright who used sound, rhythm, and imagery to convey his meanings. Consider the lines Lysander speaks to Helena when trying to persuade her that he no longer loves Hermia:

> Content with Hermia? No. I do repent
> The tedious minutes I with her have spent.
> Not Hermia but Helena I love.
> Who will not change a raven for a dove? (2.2.115-18)

In ordinary speech, someone would likely say, "I do repent the tedious minutes *I have spent with her. I love Helena, not Hermia.*" But Shakespeare's word order allows the lines to rhyme—"repent" with "spent" and "love" with "dove," giving those words special emphasis. Furthermore, the last time we heard Lysander speak in rhyming couplets, he was proclaiming his love for Hermia. His speaking in rhyming couplets to Helena—as he formerly spoke to Hermia—thus accentuates his change of heart. *(See page 73 of appendix 1 for an explanation of couplet.)*

∞ Descriptions that Provide Context. Although Shakespeare's theater included costumes and some props, it did not include sets or lighting. (The use of electricity was centuries away, and plays were performed at The Globe, an open-air theater, in the mid-afternoon.) Audiences would have to glean important context from the characters' speeches. For instance, in act 2, scene 1 of *A Midsummer Night's Dream*, Oberon describes the place where Titania sleeps:

> I know a bank where the wild thyme blows,
> Where oxlips and the nodding violet grows,
> Quite over-canopied with luscious woodbine,
> With sweet musk roses and with eglantine.
> There sleeps Titania sometime of the night,
> Lulled in these flowers with dances and delight. (2.1.249-54)

Nowadays such images could be shown to a theater audience through stage and lighting design. Thus, contemporary playwrights usually don't write such descriptions into characters' speeches, and contemporary audiences don't have to decipher and picture them.

∞ Implied Action. Unlike stories or novels, most plays don't have a narrator who tells us what characters are doing as they speak to each other. Playwrights can indicate specific actions with stage directions, but Shakespeare's plays have relatively few. Instead, the dialogue itself gives clues about characters' actions. Consider the following exchange when Lysander suddenly wants to be free of his former beloved Hermia. (*Thou* and *thee* are older forms of "you.")

Lysander	Hang off, thou cat, thou burr! Vile thing, let loose,
	Or I will shake thee from me like a serpent.
Hermia	Why are you grown so rude? What change is this?
	(3.2.260-2)

Lysander's line lets us see that Hermia is physically holding onto Lysander as he rudely rejects her. Imagining the world of a Shakespeare play depends, in part, on listening for clues to characters' actions. Try staging a scene with some friends: doing so will help you become attentive to such clues. Keep in mind that editors sometimes insert their own stage directions. *(See page 85 of appendix 3.)*

Learning to see the world of a Shakespeare play by reading or hearing its language takes some work and some patience. However, paying close attention to the play's language will give you access to the most interesting, complicated, and surprising aspects of the plays. As the Prologue to *The Life of Henry the Fifth* shows, Shakespeare invited and relied on his audiences to envision the worlds of his plays, and Shakespeare gave us incomparable language from which to do so. There are always many ways to imagine a phrase, line, or scene, but it's important to start with accurate observations of the play's language.

Using This Guide

The series of questions for each scene will help you to observe the sometimes complex and dense language accurately and to puzzle through the characters' conversations. Before trying to answer the questions for a particular scene, read through the entire scene aloud. Or, better yet, gather some friends, take parts, and read the scene aloud together. Don't be shy: you might mispronounce a word or need to read some lines slowly, but you will have a much better chance of understanding the lines when you read them aloud—and you likely will have more fun. Then, read through the scene again slowly, answering the questions as you go. If you don't fully understand a question, quote the phrase or line that you suspect contains the clues for its answer. Once you reach the scene's end, return to those questions to see if you have been able to figure out anything further.

Some of the questions use terms and refer to methods with which you may not be familiar: they may ask you to observe and analyze "meter" or "figurative language," especially "metaphor." Don't worry if you are not familiar with these terms or if you never have "scanned a line of verse" or "sorted a metaphor's tenor and vehicle": you will find the necessary background information and sample analyses in the appendices. Appendix 1, "Listening for Meter," explains how to identify the basic rhythms of Shakespeare's poetry; appendix 2, "Reading Figurative Language," explains how to identify and analyze figures of speech; and appendix 3, "On How an Edition of *A Midsummer Night's Dream* Is Made," explains how the copy of *A Midsummer Night's Dream* you are reading is derived from the earliest texts of the play and lets you know what kinds of additions and changes an editor may have made in preparing the play for publication. You may find it helpful to read through these appendices before you begin to answer the questions. Or you may consult them when you arrive at a question that requires your knowledge of the information they provide. All of the information in the appendices aims to help you to understand and envision the play for yourself.

Quotations in this guide are taken from the edition of *A Midsummer Night's Dream* edited by Burton Raffel and published by Yale University Press in 2005. Following standard scholarly practice, quotations are followed by a citation that indicates the act, scene, and lines from which a passage is quoted. So, for instance, "(3.1.6-7)" refers to act 3, scene 1, lines 6-7. If you are reading a different edition of the play, your line numbers may be slightly different. *(See appendix 3, "On How an Edition of* A Midsummer Night's Dream *Is Made," for an explanation of how the differences in editions come about.)*

Hearing & Seeing Performances

If, after trying to read aloud by yourself and with friends, you continue to have trouble getting the gist of what the characters are saying to each other, try to locate a good audio recording of the play, one that has been recorded by a cast of experienced Shakespearean actors. (Many libraries have them available.) Read along as you listen to the audio recording of the scene you are working on. Hearing trained actors deliver the characters' lines will likely help you understand much of what the characters are saying. Keep in mind that the way an actor speaks a line depends on that actor's interpretation of it and that you might have another interpretation.

After reading the play, you might enjoy seeing a performance of it. Check to see if there is a live performance at a nearby theater, or borrow a film of the play from your library. If you wait to see a performance until after reading the play, you will be able to compare the way you have imagined the play-world to the way a particular director has. If you see the performance before you've read the play, be aware, as you read, that the particular director's vision of the play is not the only possibility. If you watch two or more performances, you will probably notice significant differences in the ways different directors and actors interpret the play.

There are many books and websites that publish summaries and analyses of Shakespeare's plays. Be wary of these. Don't accept another reader's vision of the play too easily: your own careful reading and imagining might lead you to a far more interesting one!

QUESTIONS TO CONSIDER AS YOU READ *A MIDSUMMER NIGHT'S DREAM*

Note: For A Midsummer Night's Dream *Shakespeare borrowed many of his characters, names, and settings from ancient Greek myths. "Theseus," for instance, is a mythical king of Athens, and "Hippolyta" is the mythical Amazon queen whom Theseus conquers and brings back to Athens. Although Shakespeare set his play in ancient Greece with mythical Greek characters, he also included many aspects of his own Judeo-Christian, English world. For instance, Hermia can choose to be a nun if she refuses to marry Demetrius, and the woods are inhabited by local English faeries.*

Larger Questions

As you answer the questions for each scene, you often will be prompted to think about the topics listed below. If you are particularly interested in one of these topics, you might find it helpful to keep track of what various characters say about it by marking relevant passages in your text or by keeping a list of them in a notebook. When you have finished reading the play, you then will be ready to consider the collection of passages you have gathered and ask yourself what the play as a whole might be suggesting about the topic. This kind of work is one way to prepare to write an essay about *A Midsummer Night's Dream*.

1. **Eyes & Sight.** What do characters say about eyes? What powers do eyes have? What can seeing do to the one who looks? What can it do to the one who is looked at? Are there different kinds of sight?

2. **Love.** What do characters assert about the nature of love? How do characters fall in love and become lovers? What emerges about love between friends such as Hermia and Helena or Titania and the Indian boy's mother?

3. **Magic, Spells, & Charms.** What is Oberon's magic and how does it work? What about Puck's? What kinds of spells and charms do they speak? Who else uses or is said to use magic? What kinds? What other than magic is said to be enchanting or bewitching?

4. **Couples.** There are many couples in the play: Theseus and Hippolyta, Demetrius and Helena, Lysander and Hermia, Oberon and Titania. How do these various couples compare?

5. **Marriage.** What do characters assert about marriage and about how marriages should be arranged? Which idea(s) of marriage seem to hold up by the play's end?

6. **Oaths, Vows, & Promises.** Who swears an oath or makes a promise or vow? Do characters keep or break their vows? What happens when they do so? What do characters say about the nature of oaths, vows, and promises?

7. **Change & Transformation.** Look out for the many terms in the play used to describe change, including *transform, transpose, translate, transport,* and *transfigure.* Who changes and how? What forces transform characters? Which changes are considered normal? Which are considered unnatural or monstrous? At the play's end, who remains transformed? Who changes back?

8. **To Figure, Disfigure, & Transfigure.** How are these words used? Who is said to have the power to figure, disfigure, or transfigure someone or something?

9. **Dreams, Visions, & Shadows.** Only Hermia reports having a dream while sleeping. How does her dream relate to her waking life? What else do characters identify as dreams, visions, or shadows—or as like a dream? What, if anything, do characters think they can learn from dreams? What kind of dream is the dream of the play's title?

10. **Sleeping & Waking.** What does the play suggest about the relationship between sleeping and waking?

11. **Revels, Plays, Pageants, Rites, Masques, Dances, & Music.** What is the role of plays in the world of *A Midsummer Night's Dream*? What about music and dance? How are plays related to dreams and visions? About what do the workers worry as they plan to represent people, creatures, and objects in their play? What do various characters claim about plays and other arts, including stories and tales?

12. **City (Athens) & Woods.** What happens in the city? What happens in the woods? What does the play suggest is the relationship between these locations?

13. **Fairies & Mortals.** What differences are there among mortals? Between men and women? Between aristocrats and workers and craftsmen? What differences are there among the fairies? What differences are there between fairies and mortals?

14. **Reason & Imagination.** What do characters say and imply about the influence of reason? What do they say about the influence of imagination? What does the play overall suggest about reason and imagination?

15. **Concord & Discord.** What causes conflict in the natural, mortal, and fairy worlds? How do disturbances in one world affect the other worlds? How is harmony restored?

Patterns of Figurative Language

Questions for each scene will prompt you to notice and analyze figurative language. *(See appendix 2 for an introduction to figurative language.)* Sometimes one instance of figurative language echoes figurative language from other scenes in the play. These patterns of figurative language are an important part of how the play is structured and delivers its meanings. You might find it helpful to keep track of repeating figures by marking instances of them in your text or by keeping a list in a notebook. When you have finished reading the play, you then will be ready to ask yourself what the pattern suggests or means. In *A Midsummer Night's Dream*, be on the lookout for figures of:

1. **Eyes**
2. **Mind**
3. **Heart**
4. **Reason**
5. **Desire, passion**
6. **Theater, plays**
7. **Sickness, disease**
8. **Flowers**
9. **Monsters, beasts**
10. **The moon**
11. **Serpents**
12. **Storms, tempests, snow, rain**
13. **Hunting**

ACT 1, SCENE 1

1. The scene begins with Theseus speaking to Hippolyta of their upcoming wedding—their "nuptial hour" (1.1.1). How is Theseus feeling about his marriage to Hippolyta? Look for paradoxes or contradictions in what he says. Begin your answer by quoting and citing two key phrases.

2. EXTRA OPPORTUNITY. Theseus remarks that the wedding will occur on the night of the new moon—"[a]nother moon" (1.1.3). Theseus then compares his waiting to marry Hippolyta (which he will do when the "old moon" finally "wanes") to a young man waiting to inherit "revenue" (which he will do when his "stepdame or dowager" finally dies) (1.1.3-6). What does Theseus's simile imply about his marriage to Hippolyta? What does it imply about the nature of marriage?

3. What does Theseus order Philostrate to do (1.1.10-14)?

4. Explain what we learn from Theseus about how he courted Hippolyta: "I wooed thee with my sword, / And won thy love, doing thee injuries" (1.1.16-17). How did Hippolyta become Theseus's bride-to-be?

5. What does Theseus say about how, in contrast, he will wed Hippolyta?

6. Reread 1.1.7-11 ("Four days will quickly . . . Of our solemnities). What is Hippolyta's attitude toward Theseus and the wedding? With what tone do you think Hippolyta speaks these lines?

7. What complaint does Egeus bring before Theseus?

8. How, according to Egeus, has Lysander "bewitched the bosom" of Egeus's child, Hermia (1.1.27)? How has Lysander "filched" his daughter's heart (1.1.36)? (*Filched* means "stolen.") What does Egeus's choice of words suggest he thinks is Hermia's part in her relationship with Lysander?

9. What "ancient privilege of Athens" does Egeus ask Theseus to enforce (1.1.41)?

10. Theseus advises Hermia:

> To you your father should be as a god,
> One that composed your beauties, yea, and one
> To whom you are but as a form in wax,
> By him imprinted, and within his power
> To leave the figure or disfigure it. (1.1.47-51)

a. What does Theseus's first simile ("your father should be as a god") imply about how Hermia should respond to her father's wishes?

b. What does his second simile (which begins "To whom you are but as a form in wax") imply about what her father has the power to do to her?

11. What, according to Theseus, makes Demetrius a "worthier" gentleman than Lysander (1.1.55)?

12. How does Theseus respond to Hermia's wish, "I would my father looked but with my eyes" (1.1.56)? (In this sentence *would* means "wish.") Quote and explain his line.

13. Theseus tells Hermia that if she refuses to wed Demetrius, she will either "die the death" or "abjure / For ever, the society of men" (1.1.65-6). (To *abjure* means "to swear to leave for ever" [OED 3].) Theseus asks her to consider if she "can endure the livery of a nun" (1.1.70). (*Livery*, which means "distinctive dress or uniform" [OED 2b], refers here to a nun's habit or clothing.) What does Theseus emphasize about the life of a nun? Start your answer by choosing three key words in his description.

14. Consider the metaphor with which Theseus contrasts the life of a nun and a married woman:

    But earthlier happy is the rose distilled
    Than that, which withering on the virgin thorn,
    Grows, lives, and dies in single blessedness. (1.1.76-8)

    Distilling a rose into perfume preserves the essence or scent of a rose in bloom long after the rose is dead. How, does the metaphor imply, can a married woman preserve her essence? (What could a married woman leave behind even after she dies?) Fill in the tenor for the vehicle "rose essence or perfume." (*For explanations of* vehicle *and* tenor, *see pages 77-8 of appendix 2.*)

vehicle	:	tenor
rose	:	woman
distilled	:	married
withering on the thorn	:	remain a virgin nun
rose essence/perfume	:	_____

    How, then, does Theseus attempt to persuade Hermia that marrying Demetrius is better than becoming a nun?

15. Hermia announces her decision:

    > So will I grow, so live, so die, my lord,
    > Ere I will yield my virgin patent up
    > Unto his lordship, whose unwishèd yoke
    > My soul consents not to give sovereignty. (1.1.79-82)

    a. What decision has Hermia made about how she will live?

    b. EXTRA OPPORTUNITY. When Hermia refuses to marry a man without her soul's consent, what does she imply about what a woman gives up when she marries a man—even one whom she wishes to marry? What, for instance, does the metaphor of a "yoke" suggest about a wife's role even in a marriage to which she consents? What does giving "sovereignty" to a husband suggest about a wife's relationship to her husband? (A *yoke* is a device fitted to an animal so that it can pull a plough; *sovereignty* means "supreme dominion, authority, or rule" [OED 2.].)

16. Lysander asserts that he is as qualified as Demetrius to be Hermia's husband—if not more so. What does he include on his list of qualifications? What, finally, does he say "is more than all these boasts can be" (1.1.103)?

17. Of what does Lysander accuse Demetrius before calling him a "spotted and inconstant man" (1.1.110)?

18. a. What does Theseus's confession that he would have spoken to Demetrius had he not been "full of self affairs" (1.1.113) suggest about Theseus as a duke?

   b. If the "self affairs" to which Theseus refers are his own courtship of and engagement to Hippolyta, what does he suggest is the effect of wooing and love?

19. EXTRA OPPORTUNITY. After hearing the conflict over Hermia's engagement, Theseus asks Hippolyta, "what cheer, my love?" (1.1.122). Imagine what Hippolyta might have been feeling or thinking as the complaints were spoken. Then either write a private diary entry Hippolyta might write that evening, or write a stage direction describing what Hippolyta does in response to a specific line. (Be sure to indicate at what line you would insert the stage direction.)

20. Review the conversations so far (1.1.22-127). Make a list of key phrases that reveal each character's idea of how marriage should be arranged and partners determined. Be sure to consider what each character claims (or implies) is his or her privilege or right. Consider also the implications of what we learn of how Theseus's engagement to Hippolyta came about.

21. Review your list, and articulate one or two key conflicts in the ideas of marriage these characters express.

22. Reread the exchange below and notice how Hermia and Lysander speak a kind of duet and how Hermia continues her beloved Lysander's metaphor. Analyze their shared metaphor by charting its vehicle and tenor. *(For instructions on how to do so, see pages 80-3 of appendix 2.)*

> *Lysander* Why is your cheek so pale?
> How chance the roses there do fade so fast?
> *Hermia* Belike for want of rain, which I could well
> Beteem them from the tempest of my eyes. (1.1.128-31)

vehicle : tenor

23. Lysander declares that tales and history suggest that "The course of true love never did run smooth" (1.1.134). What reasons does Lysander list to explain why not?

24. Explain what Lysander means when he says, "So quick bright things come to confusion" (1.1.149).

25. How does Hermia respond to Lysander's description of how difficult love is? Quote and explain her most important phrase or line.

26. What solution does Lysander propose to their forbidden marriage?

27. EXTRA OPPORTUNITY. Note that Lysander tells Hermia: "I have a widow aunt, a dowager / Of great revenue, and she hath no child . . . And she respects me as her only son" (1.1.157-60). How do Lysander's lines echo what Theseus says to Hippolyta at the beginning of the scene? Jot down and cite the line.

28. When Hermia agrees to sneak away from her father's house—and from Athens—to marry Lysander, she swears by "Cupid's strongest bow" and "the simplicity of Venus' doves" (1.1.169-71). She also swears by "that fire which burned the Carthage queen" and by "all the vows that ever men have broke" (1.1.173-5). (The Carthage queen, Dido, killed herself when her lover Aeneas left her.)

   a. Identify and explain the paradoxes. (A *paradox* is a statement that seems self-contradictory or absurd but that turns out to be true in an unexpected way.)

   b. What is the effect of this paradoxical list of things by which Hermia swears that she will elope with Lysander?

29. Helena rejects Hermia's calling her "fair" and complains, "Demetrius loves your fair" (1.1.182). Explain what Helena means when she concludes, "Were the world mine, Demetrius being bated, / The rest I'd give to be to you translated" (1.1.190-1). (*Bate* means "to omit" or "except" [*OED* 7]; *translate* means "to transform" or "to change in form, appearance" [*OED* III.4].)

30. Helena tells Hermia, "O teach me how you look, and with what art / You sway the motion of Demetrius' heart" (1.1.192-3). What might Helena mean by "how you look"? Give two possibilities and explain what each suggests about how Helena believes a woman can "sway the motion" of a man's heart.

31. Explain Hermia's description of her life before and after seeing Lysander. Be sure to explain the paradoxes in her assertion: "Before the time I did Lysander see, / Seemed Athens as a paradise to me. / O then what graces in my love do dwell, / That he hath turned a heaven unto a hell" (1.1.204-7).

32. If you were Helena, how might you feel when Hermia tells you that she is leaving Athens? What, in particular, might be the effect of her describing the place where she will meet up with Lysander: "And in the wood, where often you and I / Upon faint primrose beds were wont to lie, / Emptying our bosoms of their counsel sweet" (1.1.214-16)?

33. Once alone, Helena speaks about Demetrius and about the nature of love. Reread Helena's speech at 1.1.226-251 ("How happy some o'er other some can be! . . . To have his sight thither and back again"). Then answer the following questions from her point of view:

   a. Why does it not matter that "Through Athens I am thought as fair as she" (1.1.227)?

   b. Explain the assertion: "Things base and vile, holding not quantity, / Love can transpose to form and dignity" (1.1.232-3).

   c. With what organ does "Love loo[k]" (1.1.234)?

   d. What oath had Demetrius made to Helena before he "looked on Hermia's eyne" (1.1.242)?

e. What does Helena expect Demetrius will do when she tells him of Hermia's flight?

f. Explain Helena's reasoning in the passage below. (Note that *intelligence* means "information.")

>   and for this intelligence
> If I have thanks, it is a dear expense.
> But herein mean I to enrich my pain,
> To have his sight thither and back again. (1.1.248-51)

ACT 1, SCENE 2

Read through the entire short scene in which Peter Quince is organizing a play to be performed "before the Duke and Duchess, on his wedding day at night" (1.2.5-6). Read aloud and, if possible, with friends who each take a part. Note that his scene is written in prose rather than in verse. *(See pages 73-4 of appendix 1 for explanations of verse and prose.)*

1. Although Quince seems to be in charge of organizing and casting the play, how does Bottom behave? Start your answer by quoting two key lines or phrases.

2. What are the occupations of the men who will be in the play? Make a list and look up any words you might not know. (For instance, *joiner* is an older word for "woodworker.") Then jot down a key phrase or two that you think particularly reveals each man's character. (I've done the first one.)

character	occupation	key phrase(s)
Quince	*carpenter*[1]	"No, no. You must play Pyramus" (1.2.49).
Bottom		
Flute		

---

[1] Quince's occupation is not mentioned in the dialogue of any scene, but he is called "Quince the Carpenter" in a stage direction that appears in each of the earliest texts of the play. *(See appendix 3 for information about the early texts.)*

character	occupation	key phrase(s)
Starveling		
Snout		
Snug		

3. List a few specific differences you notice between the way these men speak and act and the way the lords and ladies in the first scene speak and act.

4. Quince worries that if Bottom were to roar "too terribly," he "would fright the Duchess and the ladies" (1.2.66-7). What must Quince imagine about the ladies for whom they will be performing?

5. Consider the following exchange between Quince and the actors. What does Quince say would be the consequence of frightening the ladies? With what tone might Quince say his line? With what tone might the men respond? Give two possibilities.

   Quince And that were enough to hang us all.
   All   That would hang us, every mother's son. (1.2.68-9)

6. Why does Quince arrange for them to rehearse "in the palace wood" (1.2.88-9)?

7. Bottom speaks several *malapropisms*, that is, he misuses certain words by speaking a word that sounds like one that would correctly fit the meaning of the sentence. A malapropism often has a comic effect. Consider each of the malapropisms underlined below and explain the mistake in the specific context of this scene. What makes each malapropism funny?

   a. "But I will aggravate my voice so that I will roar you as gently as any sucking dove" (1.2.72-3).

   Aggravate means "To make (an offence) more heinous or offensive" (*OED* 4a). Bottom likely means *moderate*, which means, "To make less violent, severe, intense, or burdensome" (*OED* 1a).

   b. "We will meet, and there we may rehearse most obscenely and courageously" (1.2.94-5).

   Obscenely means "offensively, repulsively, horribly; indecently, lewdly" (*OED*). Bottom likely means *seemly*, which means "Fittingly, appropriately; decently" (*OED* 2).

8. Note that Bottom says: "If I do it, let the audience look to their eyes. I will move storms, I will condole in some measure" (1.2.19-21). How do Bottom's lines echo what Hermia says about storms (or tempests) and eyes in act 1, scene 1? Jot down and cite the line.

ACT 2, SCENE 1

Note: This scene includes a number of detailed descriptions of the fairy and human worlds. At the end of this scene's questions, you will be invited to illustrate one such description. As you work through the scene, keep your eyes open for details that bring a place vividly before your eyes.

1. Listen to the sound of the Fairy's response to Puck and scan the pairs of lines below. *(For an explanation of how to scan a line of verse, see page 75 of appendix 1.)*

    Over hill, over dale,

    Thorough Bush, thorough brier, (2.1.2-3)

    Those be rubies, fairy favors.

    In those freckles live their savors. (2.1.12-13)

2. What do you notice about meter and rhyme in the Fairy's speech? Do the sounds of the Fairy's speech make the Fairy seem different from the couples or the workers we met in Act 1? How so?

3. Puck tells the Fairy that the king (Oberon) will "keep his revels here tonight" and warns the Fairy to be careful not to let the queen (Titania) come "within his sight" (2.1.17-18). What explanation does Puck give about why the king Oberon is so angry—"passing fell and wrath" (2.1.20)?

4. The Fairy then recognizes Puck as "that shrewd and knavish sprite / Called Robin Goodfellow" (2.1.33-4). (*Knavish* means "mischievous" [*OED* 3].) For what mischief is Robin Goodfellow, also called "Puck," known?

5. Puck declares himself "that merry wanderer of the night" and announces, "I jest to Oberon and make him smile" (2.1.43-4). Consider the examples of his jesting Puck recounts: what special ability do we learn Puck has?

6. Of what does Titania accuse Oberon at 2.1.64-73 ("But I know / When thou hast stol'n away. . . joy and prosperity")?

7. Of what does Oberon accuse Titania at 2.1.74-80 ("How canst thou thus . . . Ariadne and Antiopa")?

8. Titania rejects Oberon's accusations as "the forgeries of jealousy" (2.1.81) and points out that they have not "since middle summer's spring" met "To dance [their] ringlets to the whistling wind" (2.1.82-6). Reread 2.1.88-114 ("Therefore the winds, piping to us in vain . . . By their increase, now knows not which is which"). What has happened to the natural and human world as a result of this disturbance in the fairy world? Start your answer by quoting a few key phrases.

9. "And this same progeny of evils comes / From our debate, from our dissension. / We are their parents and original" (2.1.115-17). (*Progeny* means "offspring" or "children" [*OED* 1.]) To what does Titania say their "debate" or argument has given birth?

10. What reason does Titania give to explain why she refuses to part with the boy for whom Oberon begs (2.1.121-37)?

11. What had Puck said about how Titania came to have the boy? (Look back at 2.1.22.)

12. Whose story—Titania's or Puck's—seems more believable to you? Why?

13. After Titania exits with her train of fairies, what does Oberon announce he will do to her?

14. What once "fell upon a little western flower" that Oberon asks Puck to fetch for him (2.1.155-69)? What special power does the juice of the flower now have (2.1.170-4)?

15. How long does Puck say it will take him to "put a girdle round about the earth" (2.1.175-6)? (A *girdle* is a belt.)

16. After Puck exits, Oberon says he will "drop the liquor" of the flower in Titania's eyes (2.1.177-8). What does he imagine she will look at next and "pursue . . . with the soul of love" (2.1.180-2)?

17. Oberon plans to "make her render up her page" to him before he removes the charm with another herb (2.1.183-5). If Oberon thinks that once Titania is pursuing some creature with "the soul of love," he will be able to acquire the boy ("her page") she has so far refused to part with, what does Oberon imply about the effect of such love?

18. When Oberon hears someone approaching, he announces, "I am invisible, / And I will overhear their conference" (2.1.186-7). Write a specific stage direction for how Oberon should perform being "invisible." Feel free to suggest more than one possibility.

19. As he rejects Helena and pursues Lysander and Hermia, Demetrius says, "The one I'll slay, the other slayeth me" (2.1.190). Explain what Demetrius means; be sure to explain the two senses of "slay."

20. Demetrius continues, "And here am I, and wode within this wood" (2.1.192). (*Wode*—a variant spelling of *wood*—can mean "out of one's mind, insane, lunatic" [*OED* 1] or "extremely rash or reckless, wild" [*OED* 2a] or "violently angry or irritated" [*OED* 3b].) What does Demetrius imply about the effect on him of his pursuit of Hermia?

21. Reread Helena's response to Demetrius's order that she follow him no more:

    > You draw me, you hard-hearted adamant.
    > But yet you draw not iron, for my heart
    > Is true as steel. Leave you your power to draw,
    > And I shall have no power to follow you. (2.1.195-8)

    Make a sketch of Helena's metaphor of Demetrius as an "adamant" that "draw[s]" her heart of steel. (An *adamant* is a magnet; *draw* means "pull" here.)

    What does Helena's metaphor imply would make her stop following Demetrius?

22. Helena continues with another simile. Reread the extended simile and chart its vehicle and tenor. (A *spaniel* is a kind of dog.)

> I am your spaniel. And, Demetrius,
> The more you beat me, I will fawn on you.
> Use me but as your spaniel, spurn me, strike me,
> Neglect me, lose me—only give me leave,
> Unworthy as I am, to follow you.
> What worser place can I beg in your love—
> And yet a place of high respect with me—
> Than to be usèd as you use your dog? (2.1.203-10)

vehicle : tenor

With what tone might Helena speak this simile? Try performing it aloud and list two or three possibilities. Which tone you would choose if you were performing the part of Helena? Why?

23. Reread what Demetrius tells Helena about her decision to follow him into the woods. (*Impeach* can mean "harm, injure" [*OED* 2].)

    > You do impeach your modesty too much,
    > To leave the city and commit yourself
    > Into the hands of one that loves you not—
    > To trust the opportunity of night
    > And the ill counsel of a desert place
    > With the rich worth of your virginity. (2.1.214-19)

    What is Demetrius advising Helena to be concerned about in "a desert place" alone with him?

24. Is Helena frightened by Demetrius's implied threat? Begin your answer by quoting and citing the line(s) from which you derive it.

25. Of what "wrongs" does Helena accuse Demetrius? How, according to Helena, do these wrongs "set a scandal on [her] sex," that is, on the female sex (2.1.240)?

26. Helena says that in following Demetrius she will "make a heaven of hell" (2.1.243). What similar remark had Hermia made about Lysander in act 1, scene 1? Quote and cite Hermia's remark. Then, compare the two situations.

27. Oberon planned to "overhear" Helena and Demetrius's "conference" while "invisible" (2.1.186-7). After they exit, for whom does Oberon express sympathy? Quote and cite the line from which you derive your answer.

28. What will Oberon do with the special flower? What does he order Puck to do?

29. Choose the passage below that most appeals to you.

    2.1.2-15: The Fairy's description of wandering
    ("Over hill, over dale . . . And hang a pearl in every cowslip's ear.")

    2.1.88-116: Titania's description of the effects on the world of her and Oberon's "debate"
    ("Therefore the winds, piping to us in vain . . . From our debate, from our dissension.")

    2.1.123-34: Titania's description of being with the Indian boy's mother
    ("His mother was a votress of my order . . . As from a voyage, rich with merchandise.")

    2.1.155-68: Oberon's description of discovering the flower with special powers
    ("That very time I saw, but thou couldst not . . . And maidens call it 'love-in-idleness'.")

    2.1.249-56: Oberon's description of where Titania will be sleeping
    ("I know a bank where the wild thyme blows . . . Weed wide enough to wrap a fairy in.") *Weed* means "garment" or "clothing" (*OED* 1, 2).

In the space below, make a list of key visual clues in your chosen passage, and then make a detailed illustration on the following blank page.

Your illustration:

ACT 2, SCENE 2

1. As she goes to sleep, what does Titania request from her fairies (2.2.1-8)?

2. What do the fairies try to ward off with their song (2.2.9-28)?

3. EXTRA OPPORTUNITY. Fairy dismisses all of the fairies except one who is appointed to stand guard: "Hence, away! . . . One aloof stand sentinel" (2.2.29-30). Oberon then approaches Titania to squeeze the magic flower juice on Titania's eyes. If you were directing the play, how would you arrange for Oberon not to be thwarted by the fairy sentinel? Write a stage direction.

4. In what meter does Oberon speak when putting the spell on Titania? Scan two lines:

    What thou see'st, when thou dost wake,

    Do it for thy true love take. (2.2.31-2)

5. Reread Lysander and Hermia's exchange at 2.2.39-69 ("Fair love, you faint with wand'ring in the wood . . . With half that wish the wisher's eyes be pressed").

   a. What reasons does Lysander give for asking to lie by Hermia's side?

   b. Explain what Lysander might mean when he concludes, "For lying so, Hermia I do not lie" (2.2.56). Be sure to explain the two meanings of lie.

   c. What reason does Hermia give for asking Lysander to "Lie further off" (2.2.61)?

6. What does Puck conclude when he sees Lysander wearing "Weeds of Athens" and Hermia "sleeping sound" (2.2.70-81)? What leads Puck to this conclusion? What does Puck do as a result?

7. What feature of Hermia's does Helena describe after asserting, "Happy is Hermia" (2.2.94-7)?

8. Explain Helena's question: "What wicked and dissembling glass of mine / Made me compare with Hermia's sphery eyne?" (2.2.102-3). (*Glass* means "mirror" here.)

9. When Helena wakes Lysander, he says, "And run through fire I will for thy sweet sake" (2.2.107). What does Helena not understand about what now influences Lysander?

10. What does Lysander imply he will do to Demetrius? Start by quoting the phrase from which you derive your answer.

11. How does Lysander explain why he now loves Helena when before he loved Hermia? What does he say about reason? What does he say about not having been "ripe" to reason until now (2.2.122)?

12. EXTRA OPPORTUNITY. Make an illustration of Lysander's two-part metaphor.

> Reason becomes the marshal to my will,
> And leads me to your eyes, where I o'erlook
> Love's stories written in love's richest book. (2.2.124-6)

13. What does Helena think is causing Lysander to say what he's saying to her?

14. Analyze Lysander's parting metaphors about Hermia and his love for her. (*Surfeit* means "Excessive consumption of food or drink" [OED 1a]; a *heresy* is an opinion held to be contrary to that of any church or religious system [OED 1a).

>   For as a surfeit of the sweetest things
>   The deepest loathing to the stomach brings
>   Or as the heresies that men do leave
>   Are hated most of those they did deceive,
>   So thou, my surfeit and my heresy,
>   Of all be hated, but the most of me. (2.2.141-8)

vehicle 1	:	vehicle 2	:	tenor
surfeit of sweetest things	:	heresies	:	

15. Considering that Lysander's change of mind and heart was induced by the magic flower juice, what does the scene invite us to wonder about Lysander's "reason"?

16. Of what had Hermia been dreaming?

17. When Hermia wakes and realizes that Lysander is gone, she proclaims, "Either death or you I'll find immediately" (2.2.160). What might make Hermia feel so desperate? (Consider the choice Theseus presented to Hermia in act 1.)

ACT 3, SCENE 1

Note: As you read this humorous scene, think about what makes you laugh. At whom or what are you laughing? Does the scene invite laughter *at* the workers-turned-amateur-actors? Do their words and deeds seem merely silly? What parts of the comedy might warrant serious consideration?

1. At the rehearsal of "Pyramus and Thisbe," Bottom worries that "the ladies cannot abide" that "Pyramus must draw a sword to kill himself" (3.1.9-10). What solution does he propose? What does this solution suggest he imagines will be too frightening for the ladies?

2. Why does Bottom insist that Snug, who will perform the lion, must "tell them plainly he is Snug the joiner" (3.1.38-9)?

3. The play's script notes that Pyramus and Thisbe meet by moonlight, and Bottom and Quince puzzle over how "to bring the moonlight into a chamber" (3.1.40-2). What does their concern reveal about their attitude toward the performance of a script? How do they solve the problem?

4. How does Bottom solve the problem of the needed wall?

5. In this scene Quince speaks a malapropism when he suggests that an actor should say he "comes to disfigure, or to present, the person of Moonshine" (3.1.51). Why would this particular mistake—*disfigure* instead of *figure*—get a laugh? What might Quince's mistake also point out about presenting or figuring something in a play?

6. Review the scene so far: what do the amateur actors' concerns indicate about how they imagine an audience experiences a play?

7. Puck asks, "What hempen homespuns have we swaggering here, / So near the cradle of the Fairy Queen?" (3.1.64-6). What is Puck's attitude toward these working men? What does his metonymy "hempen homespuns" indicate about how he judges them? (*For an explanation of metonymy, see page 84 of appendix 2.*) (*Hemp* is a plant that can be spun into cloth; *homespun* refers to a "coarse, woolen cloth" that is "spun or woven in a person's own home" [*OED* B2, A1] or to "a rustic person or peasant" who wears such cloth [*OED* B1].)

8. How would you judge Flute's performance of the part of Pyramus's lover Thisbe? Start by quoting and citing a phrase or two from which you derive your answer.

9. When Puck realizes the men are rehearsing for a play, he remarks, "I'll be an auditor—/ An actor too, perhaps, if I see cause" (3.1.67-8). How does Puck become an "actor" in the play when Bottom exits?

10. Keeping in mind that Bottom seems not to realize what has happened to his head, what funny and ironic things does he say about his friends' reaction to his transformed state? (*Dramatic irony* occurs when the audience or a character knows more than another character.) Quote one or two lines.

11. What does Quince's "Bless thee, Bottom, bless thee!" suggest about what Quince thinks caused Bottom to be "translated" into a man with ass's head (3.1.103)? Why would Bottom need a blessing?

12. When Titania wakes and hears and sees Bottom, she remarks, "Mine ear is much enamored of thy note. / So is mine eye enthrallèd to thy shape" (3.1.122-3). What has happened to Titania? (*Enthralled* means to be held captive; *shape* here means form or figure, that is, what he looks like.)

13. What does Bottom say about the relationship between reason and love? Quote the line. Who has said something similar?

14. How does Bottom respond to Titania's compliments and professions of love? Quote one or two key phrases. Then explain what these responses indicate about Bottom's character.

15. How does Bottom address the fairies who introduce themselves to him?

16. EXTRA OPPORTUNITY. Choose what Bottom says either to Cobweb, Peaseblossom, or Mustardseed. Quote and explain it:

17. EXTRA OPPORTUNITY. After Titania commands the fairies to lead Bottom to her bower, she says:

> The moon, methinks, looks with a wat'ry eye,
> And when she weeps, weeps every little flower,
> Lamenting some enforcèd chastity. (3.1.177-9)

Although editor Burton Raffel explains *enforcèd chastity* as "violated virginity, forced rape," this explanation doesn't fit easily with the words' definitions. Here are *The Oxford English Dictionary*'s definitions of key words:

- *enforcèd*: "1. That is subjected to force or constraint. 2. That is forced upon or exacted from a person; that is produced by force; forced, constrained" (*OED* 1, 2)
- *chastity*: "purity from unlawful sexual intercourse" or "abstinence from all sexual intercourse; virginity" (*OED* 1, 2).
- *lament*: "To express profound sorrow for; to mourn" (*OED* 1).

How would you explain why, according to Titania, the moon and flowers weep, "Lamenting some enforcèd chastity"? Be sure to include your explanation of the phrase. What does Titania imply the moon wishes for the world?

18. Titania orders the fairies attending her: "Tie up my lover's tongue, bring him silently" (3.1.180). If you were directing the play, how would you stage this moment? What would Bottom be doing? How would the fairies tie up his tongue? Explain your idea either by writing a detailed stage direction or making a sketch of this moment in the scene.

ACT 3, SCENE 2

1. Reread Puck's description of how his mistress (Titania) came to be in love with a "monster" (3.2.6-34) and answer the following questions:

    a. Consider: "A crew of patches, rude mechanicals, / That work for bread upon Athenian stalls" (3.2.9-10). What is Puck's attitude toward the men and toward the kind of work they do? (*Patch* means "fool" or "clown" [*OED* 1]; *rude* can mean "slow-witted" or "uneducated" [*OED* 1b, 3]; *mechanical* is an older name for someone who does manual work [*OED* A1, B1.])

    b. Analyze the simile with which Puck describes how Bottom's fellow-actors "fly." (A *fowler* is a hunter of birds; a *chough* is a bird; the *gun's report* would be the sound of the hunter's gun; to *fly* can mean to take wing or to run away.)

    > When they him spy,
    > As wild geese that the creeping fowler eye,
    > Or russet-pated choughs, many in sort,
    > Rising and cawing at the gun's report,
    > Sever themselves and madly sweep the sky.
    > So, at his sight, away his fellows fly. (3.2.19-24)

vehicle	:	tenor
geese or choughs	:	_____
fowler (and his gun's report)	:	_____
rise, caw, sever, sweep	:	_____

    c. Explain what Puck says about what fear caused the men to experience:

    > Their sense thus weak, lost with their fears thus strong,
    > Made senseless things begin to do them wrong. (3.2.27-8)

    How did their fear affect their sense? What were the "senseless things" that began to "do them wrong"? Quote at least one specific "senseless thing" Puck mentions.

2. How does Oberon respond to Puck's report?

3. When Oberon and Puck see Hermia and Demetrius, what does Puck realize?

4. What does Hermia suspect Demetrius has done?

5. In what way does Demetrius feel "murdered" by Hermia (3.2.58-60)?

6. What comparison does Hermia make when she asks Demetrius, "Could not a worm, an adder, do so much?" (3.2.71).

7. EXTRA OPPORTUNITY. Analyze and explain the metaphor Demetrius speaks when he decides to cease following Hermia and to stop for the night. What relationship does he suggest between sorrow and sleep? What do the vehicles of debt, bankruptcy, pay, and tender imply about sleep and sorrow? (*Tender* can mean "an offer of money" [*OED* n.2 1b].)

> So sorrow's heaviness doth heavier grow.
> For debt that bankrupt sleep doth sorrow owe,
> Which now in some slight measure it will pay,
> If for his tender here I make some stay. (3.2.84-7)

vehicle : tenor

8. Oberon scolds Puck for his mistake—"misprision"—with the love juice, which, he says, "must perforce ensue / Some true love turned, and not a false turned true" (3.2.90-1). How, then, does Oberon perceive Lysander's love for Helena?

9. Explain Puck's response: "Then fate o'errules, that, one man holding troth, / A million fail, confounding oath on oath" (3.2.92-3). What, according to Puck, is the fate of oaths of love? What similar remark has Hermia made?

10. What new command does Oberon give Puck?

11. When Oberon squeezes the magic love juice in the sleeping Demetrius's eyes, he says, "When his love he doth espy, / Let her shine as gloriously / As the Venus of the sky" (3.2.105-7). Who is "his love"? What does Oberon imply about why Demetrius has rejected Helena?

12. When Puck asks "Shall we their fond pageant see" (3.2.114), to what does he refer? (*Pageant* is another word for a play.) Sort the metaphor's vehicle and tenor.

vehicle	:	tenor
pageant	:	_____
_____	:	Helena and Lysander

    What does this metaphor imply about Puck's attitude toward the mortal world?

13. What "sport" (3.2.119) does Puck look forward to? (*Sport* here means "entertainment" [*OED* 1].)

14. What does Helena say about vows and oaths (3.2.130-3)? Sketch the image: "Your vows to her and me, put in two scales, / Will even weigh, and both as light as tales."

15. When Demetrius wakes, he addresses Helena as "goddess, nymph, perfect" (3.2.137). What does he then go on to say? What comparisons does he make?

16. How does Helena respond? What does she conclude Demetrius and Lysander both are doing?

17. Lysander tells Demetrius, "In Hermia's love I yield you up my part" and asks Demetrius to "bequeath" to him his love of Helena (3.2.165-6). What does this declaration and request reveal about how Lysander imagines men's relationships with the women they love? (*Yield* here means "to give as due" or "to give back" [*OED* 2, 4]; *bequeath* means "to make a formal assignation of property" [*OED* 4].)

18. Analyze the metaphor with which Demetrius explains his love for Helena. (*Sojourn* means "to make a temporary stay in a place" [*OED* 1a] or "to be a lodger in another's house" [*OED* 1c].)

>   If e'er I loved her, all that love is gone.
>   My heart to her but as guest-wise sojourned,
>   And now to Helen it home returned,
>   There to remain. (3.2.170-3)

vehicle   :   tenor

19. EXTRA OPPORTUNITY. Make a sketch of the metaphor.

20. When Hermia arrives, Lysander asks her, "Could not this make thee know / The hate I bear thee made me leave thee so?" (3.2.189-90). How does Helena respond? Of what does she accuse Hermia?

21. When Helena recounts for Hermia their "school days' friendship" (3.2.201-14), to what does she compare the two of them. Make a list:

22. EXTRA OPPORTUNITY.

   a. How does Helena explain how she and Hermia were "like two artificial gods" (3.2.203)? (*Artificial* here means "skilled in art" [*OED* 9b].)

   b. In act 1, whom had Theseus compared to a god?

46

23. Explain what Helena means when she concludes: "Our sex, as well as I, may chide you for it, / Though I alone do feel the injury" (3.2.218-19). What does Helena feel is an offense to their "sex," that is, to women?

24. Does Hermia imagine, as Helena does, that Lysander is professing his love for Helena to scorn her? Quote and cite the line from which you derive your answer.

25. What does Lysander suggest he could do to prove to Demetrius his hate of Hermia?

26. Explain Hermia's questions, "Am I not Hermia? Are not you Lysander?" (3.2.273).

27. Once Hermia is convinced that Lysander does not jest but actually hates her, of what does she accuse Helena?

28. a. Jot down clues in the text about Hermia and Helena's fight. What names, for instance, do they call each other? What do their lines suggest they are doing physically?

b. Then, imagine you are directing the scene and write brief directions for the two actors.

29. How does Helena eventually explain to Hermia why she did not keep her counsel and told Demetrius of Hermia's "stealth unto this wood" (3.2.310)?

30. As you reread the instructions Oberon gives to Puck at 3.2.354-69 ("Thou see'st, these lovers . . . with wonted sight"), make a list of important clues for:

   a. how to design the stage and lighting in a modern theater

   b. how to direct Puck to act when later he follows Oberon's instructions

31. Why does Oberon want Puck to incite Demetrius and Lysander to fight?

32. Oberon gives Puck an herb to "crush . . . into Lysander's eye" and explains its "liquor hath this virtuous property, / To take from thence all error with his might, / And make his eyeballs roll with wonted sight" (3.2.366-9). What does Oberon suggest about Lysander's pursuit of Helena? (*Wonted* means "customary, usual" [*OED* II3].)

33. What, according to Oberon, shall "all this derision" seem like to the lovers "When next they awake" (3.2.370-1)?

34. What will Oberon do while Puck is restoring harmony among the lovers?

35. Why, according to Puck, must they act with haste? What does Puck describe happens as the dawn, "Aurora," approaches (3.2.380-4)?

36. What evidence does Oberon give for his assertion, "But we are spirits of another sort" (3.2.388)?

37. Review Oberon's instructions at 3.2.360-2 ("Like to Lysander sometime frame thy tongue. . . . And sometime rail thou like Demetrius"). Then, write a stage direction for how Puck should say the following lines:

"Here, villain, drawn and ready. Where art thou?" (3.2.402)

stage direction:

"Ho, ho ho! Coward, why com'st thou not?" (3.2.406)

stage direction:

38. Once Lysander, Demetrius, Helena, and Hermia have decided to sleep for the night, Puck applies to Lysander's eyes the herb that Oberon has given him. What does Puck say as he does so (3.2.448-57)? Quote key words in your summary of Puck's charm.

39. Note that Oberon does not order Puck to treat Demetrius's eyes with this error-correcting herb. What does Oberon's decision suggest is his view of Demetrius's love for Helena?

40. Review the charms with which Oberon and Puck anoint the eyes of Lysander, Titania, Demetrius and those with which they reverse the charms on the eyes of Lysander and Titania. Note similarities and differences. What ideas do the charms suggest about sight and attraction?

ACT 4, SCENE 1

As you reread the opening of the scene, notice that Bottom doesn't seem to realize that he's been "translated" into a man with an ass's head and that Titania doesn't seem to realize that her new lover is a man with an ass's head.

1. Review 4.1.1-50 ("Come sit thee down . . . With coronet of fresh and fragrant flowers") and jot down clues for Bottom's costume and makeup. Then describe or sketch your idea for Bottom's costume and makeup design.

2. For each of the passages below, write a detailed stage direction—one for Titania and one for Bottom—that suggests what the actors could do to help convey the humor that ensues.

    Titania   Come sit thee down upon this flowery bed,
                   While I thy amiable cheeks do coy,
                   And stick mush roses in thy sleek smooth head,
                   And kiss thy fair large ears, my gentle joy. (4.1.1-4)

    stage direction:

Mustardseed	What's your will?
Bottom	Nothing, good mounsieur, but to help Cavalery Cobweb to scratch. I must to the barber's, mounsieur, for methinks I am marvelous hairy about the face, and I am such a tender ass, if my hair do but tickle me, I must scratch. (4.1.21-5)

stage direction:

3. How does Bottom speak to the fairies that Titania has wait on him? Start your answer by quoting one or two of Bottom's phrases or lines.

4. As Oberon and Puck look on the sleeping Titania and Bottom, Oberon recounts meeting Titania and then gives Puck his next orders. Reread Oberon's speech at 4.1.44-68 ("Welcome, good Robin . . . But first I will release the fairy queen") and then answer the following according to Oberon's account:

   a. How does Oberon now feel when seeing Titania dote on Bottom (4.1.44-5)?

   b. For what did Oberon "upbraid" Titania (4.1.46-50)? (*Upbraid* means "To reproach, reprove, censure" [OED 2].)

   c. What does Oberon say the dew "which sometime on the buds / Was wont to swell like round and orient pearls" was instead like? (4.1.51-4). What does he suggest makes it so?

d. Oberon says that when he had "taunted" (or reproached) Titania for being with Bottom, she "begged [his] patience" (4.1.55-6). If Titania had begged Oberon's patience (or tolerance) how must she have felt, at that point, about being with Bottom? (*Taunt* means "To reproach a person . . . in a sarcastic, scornful, or insulting way" [*OED* 3]; *patience* means "Patient endurance or tolerance *of* something" [*OED* 3 *Obs.*].)

e. When Oberon asks for "her changeling child," Titania "straight" gave him to Oberon (4.1.57-9). If Titania gave up the boy so easily at this point, what can you infer makes her forget her previous fiercely felt obligation to the boy's mother?

f. What does Oberon announce that he will do now that he has the boy?

g. What does he instruct Puck to do?

h. What does Oberon plan for Bottom to think "of this night's accidents" (4.1.66)? (In Shakespeare's day, *accident* could mean "An occurrence, incident, event" [*OED* 5b].) Quote the key phrase Oberon uses.

5. When Titania wakes, how does she understand her night with Bottom?

6. Where must Bottom be at the moment Oberon says, "There lies your love" (4.1.76)?

7. How might Titania be feeling when Oberon shows her the sleeping Bottom, whom he calls "her love" (4.1.76)? With what tone might Titania ask, "How came these things to pass?" (4.1.76)? Give two possibilities.

8. a. What does Oberon tell Titania will happen "Now [that] thou and I are new in amity" (4.1.86)? (*Amity* means "friendly relations" [*OED*]).

   b. What does Oberon thereby suggest is the relationship between the fairy and the mortal worlds?

9. Why does Theseus call for the "forester" (4.1.102)? What is he planning now that their "observation" (4.1.103) is performed?

10. Note how the transition between scenes is emphasized by a change of music. What kind of music had Titania called for (4.1.81)? What kind of "music" does Theseus look forward to (4.1.105, 109-10)? (Hounds are used in hunting.)

11. What hunting story does Hippolyta tell? With what paradoxes does she describe the sounds of it? Quote and cite the phrases.

12. a. How does Theseus respond when Egeus wonders about the sleeping Hermia, Lysander, Demetrius, and Helena "being here together" (4.1.131)?

   b. Consider that Theseus greets them by saying, "Good morrow, friends. Saint Valentine is past. /Begin these woodbirds but to couple now" (139-40). Then suggest two possible reasons why Theseus might respond to Egeus as he does.

13. How does Lysander respond to Theseus's question, "How comes this gentle concord in the world" (4.1.143)?

14. How, according to Egeus, would Lysander and Hermia's flight have "defeated" him and Demetrius (4.1.154-9)?

15. Demetrius speaks a metaphor and a simile to explain what happened to his previous love for Hermia. Analyze each figure by sorting its vehicle and tenor. (*Idle* means "void of meaning or sense; foolish" [*OED* 2b]; a *gaud* is a "game, sport, or pastime" [*OED* 1a]; *dote* means "to bestow excessive love or fondness *on* or *upon*" [*OED* 3].)

                        my love to Hermia
Melted as the snow   (4.1.165-6)

    <u>vehicle</u>   :   <u>tenor</u>

                      my love to Hermia . . .
                      seems to me now
As the remembrance of an idle gaud
Which in my childhood I did dote upon (4.1.165-8)

    <u>vehicle</u>   :   <u>tenor</u>

What do Demetrius's metaphor and simile imply about love?

16. Demetrius then speaks a simile to explain how he now once again loves Helena, to whom he was bethrothed before he saw Hermia. Analyze the simile.

> The object and the pleasure of mine eye,
> Is only Helena. To her, my lord,
> Was I betrothed, ere I saw Hermia.
> But like a sickness, did I loathe this food.
> But, as in health, come to my natural taste,
> Now I do wish it, love it, long for it,
> And will for evermore be true to it. (4.1.170-6)

vehicle	:	tenor
sickness	:	
loathe	:	
food	:	
health	:	
natural taste	:	

17. How does Theseus respond? What does he say to Egeus? What happens to the hunting plans? Where will they go "Three and three" (4.1.184)?

18. How do the lovers feel about what has happened? Quote two or three phrases that you think contain the most important clues.

19. What does Bottom's first line upon waking—"When my cue comes, call me, and I will answer" (4.1.200)—indicate about where he thinks he is and what he thinks is happening around him? (A *cue* is "[t]he concluding . . . words of a speech in a play, serving as a signal . . . to another actor to enter, or begin his speech" [*OED* n.2, 1].)

20. Bottom then observes that he has had "a most rare vision" (4.1.204). What does Bottom decide about trying to explain his vision or dream with words? What does he decide to "get Peter Quince" to do instead (4.1.212)?

21. What reason does Bottom give that it shall be called "Bottom's Dream"?

22. EXTRA OPPORTUNITY. As many scholars have noted, in his commentary, Bottom misquotes the Bible's Book of 1 Corinthians. What do you notice about his misquoting?

    Here's 1 Corinthians 2:9 in the 1560 Geneva Bible:

    > But as it is written, The things which eye hath not seen, neither ear hath heard, neither came into man's heart, are, which God hath prepared for them that love him.

    And here's what Bottom says at 4.1.209-12:

    > The eye of man hath not heard, the ear of man hath not seen, man's hand is not able to taste, his tongue to conceive, nor his heart to report, what my dream was.

23. Compare the reactions of those who wake up after the night in the woods—Titania, Lysander, Demetrius, Helena, Hermia, and Bottom. What does each say? Do you think Puck's idea that Bottom is particularly foolish—more so than the other mortals—holds true? Why or why not?

ACT 4, SCENE 2

1. When Quince asks if Bottom has "come home yet," Starveling responds, "Out of doubt he is transported" (4.2.1-4). Considering the context, what does Starveling mean by "transported" here?

2. Why, according to the other men, "is the play marred" if Bottom "come not" (4.2.5)? (*Marred* means "ruined.")

3. Reread this part of the exchange about Bottom: and note Quince's malapropism:

   Quince [H]e is a very paramour for a sweet voice.
   Flute You must say paragon. A paramour is, God bless us, a thing of naught. (4.2.11-14).

   Quince mistakenly says *paramour*, which means "lover," (*OED* 2a) instead of *paragon*, which means "a person who serves as a model of some quality" (*OED* 1). How does Quince's malapropism add irony and humor? Hint: what do we, the audience, know about Bottom's recent adventures that his friends don't know?

4. What do Snug and Flute say would have happened "If [their] sport had gone forward" (4.2.16-17)? (*Sport* here means "entertainment" [*OED* 1].)

5. What does Bottom tell the men about his experience since he last saw them? What does he not tell them?

6. When Bottom tells the men to get ready because the "Duke hath dined" and their "play is preferred," he orders, "let not him that plays the lion pare his nails, for they shall hang out for the lion's claws" (4.2.30-5). What does Bottom's direction show about his sense of how to represent a character in a play?

7. Bottom then orders, "And most dear actors, eat no onions nor garlic. For we are to utter sweet breath. And I do not doubt to hear them say, it is a sweet comedy" (4.2.36-8). Do you think Bottom is making a pun on "sweet"? If not, explain why not. If so, explain how the pun works.

A pun is the use of a word in a statement that simultaneously suggests two or more meanings of the word and, thus, two or more ways to understand the statement.

ACT 5, SCENE 1

1. The scene begins with Hippolyta remarking, "'Tis strange my Theseus, that these lovers speak of" (5.1.1). What would "these lovers"—Demetrius, Helena, Lysander, and Hermia—have been speaking of?

2. Theseus counters that what the lovers speak of is "more strange than true" (5.1.2). He compares lovers to madmen and poets as he explains why he doesn't believe their story. Answer the following questions according to what Theseus asserts in his speech at 5.1.2-22 ("More strange than true . . . How easy is a bush supposed a bear?"):

   a. What do the "seething brains" of "lovers and madmen" do (5.1.4-6)?

   b. If the imagination of the "lunatic, the lover, and the poet" are "all compact," what do they have in common (5.1.7-8)?

   c. How is the lunatic who "sees more devils than vast hell can hold" like the lover who "Sees Helen's beauty in a brow of Egypt" (5.1.9-11)? *(Note: Helen was a famous Greek beauty; Theseus implies that a woman from Egypt could not be as beautiful.)*

   d. What specifically does "the poet's pen" do "as imagination bodies forth / The forms of things unknown" (5.1.12-17)? Quote Theseus's phrase and then put it into your own words.

e. Explain Theseus's assertion about "strong imagination": "That if it would but apprehend some joy, / It comprehends some bringer of that joy" (5.1.18-20)? (*Apprehend* can mean "To feel emotionally" [*OED* 7]; *comprehend* can mean "To grasp with the mind" and also "to include" [*OED* II4a, III].) Hint: does Theseus seem to think there's necessarily a tangible "bringer" of the joy apprehended or felt?

f. How can "imagining some fear" at night affect a person (5.1.21)?

g. How would you sum up Theseus's argument? Complete this sentence:

Theseus thinks lunatics, lovers, and poets are similar because they all _____

_____

_____.

3. Explain what Hippolyta says to refute Theseus's disbelief:

> But all the story of the night told over,
> And all their minds transfigured so together,
> More witnesseth than fancy's images,
> And grows to something of great constancy. (5.1.23-6)

What, for Hippolyta, "more witnesseth"—or provides evidence—that there is more to the lovers' talk than "fancy's images"? (*Fancy* is another word for "fantasy" or "imagination.")

4. Do you think the play as a whole supports Theseus's or Hippolyta's assessment? Derive your answer from a specific observation of the text.

5. Theseus asks Philostrate what masques, dances, or music he has for the evening to "wear away this long age of three hours, / Between our after supper and bedtime" (5.1.33-4). He adds, "How shall we beguile / The lazy time, if not with some delight" (5.1.41-2)? How would "lazy" time act? What would beguiling—or deceiving—lazy time do to it? What is Theseus's idea of what entertainment is for? (*Beguile* means to "deceive" or "cheat" [*OED* 1].)

6. When Theseus chooses "A tedious brief scene of young Pyramus / And his love Thisbe, very tragical mirth" (5.1.57-8), what does Philostrate say about the men who "play it" (5.1.72-6)? What does Philostrate say about the play as he tries to talk Theseus out of choosing it (5.1.78-83)?

7. EXTRA OPPORTUNITY. Theseus chooses the play despite Philostrate's critique and Hippolyta's reluctance. He explains how he has seen clerks "shiver and look pale" and "in their fears" not be able to speak their planned welcome before him, the Duke (5.1.97-9). Theseus explains:

> Out of this silence, yet, I picked a welcome.
> And in the modesty of fearful duty
> I read as much, as from the rattling tongue
> Of saucy and audacious eloquence.
> Love, therefore, and tongue-tied simplicity
> In least speak most, to my capacity. (5.1.102-7)

What, in sum, does Theseus say is more important than eloquent speech? What claim does he make about being able to understand intention when speech fails a fearful subject?

8. What is the purpose of Quince's prologue? (What had he and the other players most worried about when preparing to perform for the Duke?)

9. How do Theseus, Lysander, and Hippolyta respond to Quince? Quote one or two remarks and indicate with what tone would you direct the actor to say it.

10. Analyze Lysander's simile by sorting its vehicle and tenor: "He hath rid his prologue like a rough colt." (5.1.121). (*Rid* here is short for "ridden.")

   vehicle   :   tenor

11. Reread:

    Theseus   I wonder if the lion be to speak.
    Demetrius   No wonder, my lord. One lion may, when many asses do. (5.1.153-4)

    First explain what Demetrius means, and then explain what he doesn't understand his response would mean to the audience of *A Midsummer Night's Dream* that was privy to Bottom's transformation.

12. What does Snout explain in his first speech (5.1.155-64)? What would an actor have to imagine about a play's audience to feel it necessary to give such an explanation before the action of the play begins?

13. EXTRA OPPORTUNITY. Notice the rhyme and repetition in Bottom's first speech as Pyramus. How does the language of the play "Pyramus and Thisbe" compare to the language of *A Midsummer Night's Dream*?

14. EXTRA OPPORTUNITY. Although there is no stage direction in any early text of the play, many editors of modern editions add a stage direction after Bottom-as-Pyramus says to Snout-as-Wall, "Show me thy chink, to blink through with mine eyne!" (5.1.176). Yale editor Burton Raffel indicates, "Snout stretches out his fingers." Cambridge editor R. A. Foakes indicates, "Wall parts his fingers." In their earlier rehearsal, when Bottom insisted that some man must present Wall, he specified, "let him hold his fingers thus. And through that cranny shall Pyramus and Thisbe whisper" (3.1.56-9). However, during the performance, Snout describes the chink: "And this the cranny is, right and sinister" (5.1.163). (*Sinister* means "left.")

How would you stage how Snout-as-Wall, forms the "chink" or "cranny"? What other body parts could be arranged "right and sinister" to make the chink? If he does hold his fingers, how would he hold them "right and sinister"? Make a quick sketch of two possibilities of Wall making the chink. (You might consider the clues in Flute-as-Thisby's possibly obscene lines, "I kiss the wall's hole" (5.1.201) and "My cherry lips have often kissed thy stones" (5.1.189)!)

15. Reread:

> *Theseus* The wall, methinks, being sensible, should curse again.
> *Bottom* No, in truth, sir, he should not. "Deceiving me" is Thisbe's cue. She is to enter now.
> (5.1.181-4)

How does Bottom understand Theseus's comment? How do you think Theseus intends it?

16. Note that Bottom-as-Pyramus again mixes up senses: "I see a voice. Now will I to the chink, / To spy and I can hear my Thisbe's face" (5.1.191-2). How might it make some sense for Bottom to say here that he "see[s] a voice"?

17. What do Theseus and Hippolyta say about imagination now (5.1.211-15)?

18. EXTRA OPPORTUNITY. Sketch Theseus's metaphor: "The iron tongue of midnight hath told twelve" (5.1.351). (As you plan your sketch, you might consider that in Shakespeare's day, clocks chimed on the hour.)

19. Did the play accomplish Theseus's original goal "To wear away this long age of three hours, / Between our after supper and bedtime" (5.1.33-4)? Quote the phrase from which you derive your answer.

20. How does Puck describe "the time of night" (5.1.359-78)? Quote the parts of his description you find most striking.

21. Oberon and Titania, and their attending fairies, bless the house. Reread Oberon's blessing of the "bride-bed" and the "issue" of the couples (5.1.391-402). (*Issue* means "child.") What does the blessing ensure about the married couples and their children? Start your answer by quoting key phrases.

22. Reread Puck's final speech, which is spoken to the audience of *A Midsummer Night's Dream*. It is at 5.1.411-26 ("If we shadows have offended . . . And Robin shall restore amends"). (In Shakespeare's day, *shadow* was another word for *actor*.)

   a. What does Puck advise audience members to do "if we shadows have offended" (5.1.411)?

   b. For what does Puck imagine needing the audience's "pardon" (5.1.418)?

   c. When Puck commands, "Give me your hands" (5.1.425), he likely is asking the audience to clap—to applaud. What does Puck promise in exchange for the audience's applause?

   d. How many times does Puck use the word "if"?

   e. What does Puck's speech suggest about the relationship between actors and audience?

   f. What does Puck say is "No more yielding but a dream" (5.1.416)? (Here *but* means "than"; *yielding* means "productive" [OED 2].)

   g. By the end of *A Midsummer Night's Dream*, have visions and dreams yielded anything? If so, what?

APPENDIX 1. LISTENING FOR METER—AN INTRODUCTION

Actors have long observed that Shakespeare's plays convey their meanings not only through the sense of his language but also through its sounds, including rhyme, alliteration (repeated consonant sounds), and assonance (repeated vowel sounds). As you read the play, read speeches aloud and consider how the sounds contribute to their meanings.

This section will help you get started listening for the rhythms of a Shakespeare play by introducing you to meters you will encounter in *A Midsummer Night's Dream*.

> ❧ For most English literature, **METER** refers to a deliberate pattern of stressed and unstressed syllables.
>
> *"Stressed" syllables are the syllables that get the most emphasis when a word or sentence is spoken aloud. (In the literature of some other languages, including Greek and Latin, meter is measured by the length rather than the stress of syllables.)*
>
> *Keep in mind that you can hear the meter in which a poet has composed a speech or poem even while you can hear how the poet has, at times, varied that meter.*
>
> ❧ In a Shakespeare play, speeches in **VERSE** are composed with a repeating pattern of stressed and unstressed syllables and are divided into deliberate lines. Shakespeare's verse is composed in meter.
>
> ❧ In a Shakespeare play, speeches in **PROSE** are composed without a repeating pattern of stressed and unstressed syllables and are not divided into deliberate lines. Prose is not composed in meter.

Examples of VERSE in *A Midsummer Night's Dream*:

> *Hippolyta*   Four days will quickly steep themselves in night,
>   Four nights will quickly dream away the time,
>   And then the moon, like to a silver bow
>   New bent in heaven, shall behold the night
>   Of our solemnities. (1.1.7-11)
>
> *Quince*   Let Lion, Moonshine, Wall, and lovers twain,
>   At large discourse, while here they do remain. (5.1.151-2)

> ❧ *Quince's speech above, two lines that have the same meter and that rhyme, is called a* **COUPLET**.

- When you are reading Shakespeare's verse, you will see that the first word of each new line of a speech is capitalized whether or not it begins a new sentence.

- Whatever the size of a book's pages, printers retain the lines of a speech in verse. Thus, often you will see empty space between the end of a line and the right margin of your book's page. If a line of verse is longer than what fits on a particular page, then what remains of the verse line usually is indented and printed directly below.

- When you quote verse, you should retain the capital letters and indicate the line breaks with a forward slash, called a *virgule*. Example: When Theseus complains that the time until their wedding is passing slowly, Hippolyta predicts, "Four days will quickly steep themselves in night, / Four nights will quickly dream away the time" (1.1.7-8).

An example of PROSE in *A Midsummer Night's Dream*:

> Bottom   I see their knavery. This is to make an ass of me, to fright me, if they could. But I will not stir from this place, do what they can. I will walk up and down here, and I will sing, that they shall hear I am not afraid. (3.1.104-7)

- When you are reading prose, you will see that lines are printed until a word nearly reaches the right margin of the page. The first word of a new line, which varies depending on the size of the book, is not capitalized unless it happens to begin a new sentence.

❧ An **IAMB** is a poetic foot of one unstressed syllable (marked "˘") followed by one stressed syllable (marked "/"). Examples of single words that are iambs are:

$$\breve{re}\acute{hearse} \qquad \breve{con}\acute{sent} \qquad \breve{ap}\acute{pear}$$

❧ **IAMBIC PENTAMETER** names the meter of a line of verse with five ("penta") iambs. An example:

$$\breve{The}\ \acute{ox}\ \breve{hath}\ \acute{therefore}\ \breve{stretched}\ \acute{his}\ \breve{yoke}\ \acute{in}\ \breve{vain}\ (2.1.93)$$

❧ **IAMBIC DIMETER** names the meter of a line of verse with two ("di") iambs. An example:

> But stay. O spite!
> But mark, poor knight, (5.1.269-70)

   ❧ *The above lines are another example of a COUPLET—two rhyming lines with the same meter.*

🙢 Marking the stressed and unstressed syllables of a line of verse in the manner above is called **SCANSION**. To **SCAN** a line of verse is to listen for and mark its stressed and unstressed syllables and to notice what kind and how many of the repeating foot make up the line. Scansion also includes noticing any variations in the meter of a line. *(See page 76 for examples of variations in iambic pentameter.)*

Sometimes a line of verse is spoken by more than one character. Here is a single iambic pentameter line shared by Fairy and Puck:

Fairy   ˘ / ˘ /
         Are not you he?

Puck   ˘ / ˘ /
                              Thou speak'st aright, (2.1.42)

Note that the contraction of "speakest" as "speak'st" becomes one stressed syllable and keeps the meter of the line. Also note that Puck's speech is indented to show that it finishes Fairy's line.

And here is a single iambic pentameter line shared by Hermia and Helena:

Hermia   ˘ / ˘ /
           Do you not jest?

Helena   ˘ / ˘ / ˘ /
                              Yes, sooth, and so do you. (3.2.265)

Note that Helena's speech is indented to show that it finishes Hermia's line.

🙢 A **TROCHEE** is a poetic foot of one stressed syllable followed by one unstressed syllable. Examples of single words that are trochees are:

   / ˘   / ˘   / ˘
  mortal   fairy   moonbeams

🙢 **TROCHAIC TETRAMETER** names the meter of a line with four ("tetra") trochees. Examples:

/ ˘ / ˘ / ˘ / ˘
If we shadows have offended,
/ ˘ / ˘ / ˘ / ˘
Think but this, and all is mended: (5.1.411-12)

  _ *The above lines are another example of a COUPLET—two rhyming lines with the same meter.*

/ ˘ / ˘ / ˘ /
That you have but slumbered here,
/ ˘ / ˘ / ˘ /
While these visions did appear. (5.1.413-14)

     🙢 *The meter of these last two lines, which lack the unstressed syllable of their final trochee, is named* ***CATALECTIC TROCHAIC TETRAMETER.***

🌿 An **ANAPEST** is a poetic foot of two unstressed syllables followed by one stressed syllable. Examples of single words that are anapests are:

      ˇ ˇ /   ˇ ˇ /   ˇ ˇ /
comprehend   undergo   overbear

🌿 **ANAPESTIC DIMETER** names the meter of a line with two ("di") anapests. Example:

    ˇ ˇ / ˇ ˇ /
    Over hill, over dale,
        ˇ ˇ / ˇ ˇ /
        Thorough bush, thorough brier,
    ˇ ˇ / ˇ ˇ /
    Over park, over pale,
        ˇ ˇ / ˇ ˇ /
        Thorough flood, thorough fire. (2.1.2-5)

Although much of *A Midsummer Night's Dream* is composed in iambic pentameter, you will hear many variations in the meter. Below are two to listen for. When you notice a variation, consider what its sound adds to a speech's meanings.

🌿 Some iambic lines end with an extra unstressed syllable. Such a line is said to have a **FEMININE ENDING**. An example of an iambic pentameter line with a feminine ending:

    ˇ / ˇ / ˇ / ˇ / ˇ / ˇ
    His mother was a votress of my order, (2.1.123)

🌿 Some iambic lines substitute a trochee for one of the iambs. Here's an example of an iambic pentameter line that begins with a **TROCHEE SUBSTITUTION**:

    / ˇ ˇ / ˇ / ˇ / ˇ /
    These are the forgeries of jealousy. (2.1.81)

APPENDIX 2. READING FIGURATIVE LANGUAGE—
AN INTRODUCTION TO METAPHOR, SIMILE, METONYMY, & SYNECDOCHE

Shakespeare's plays are famous for their figures of speech, which are rich in meaning and sometimes difficult to understand. What follows is an introduction to four key figures of speech—metaphor, simile, metonymy, and synecdoche—along with some techniques you can use as you work to understand them.

> ❧ A **METAPHOR** asserts that one thing is another thing and demands that we imagine how it can be so.

> "A rose is a flower" is not a metaphor. A rose is **LITERALLY** a flower. Anyone could find this out by looking up "rose" in a dictionary.

> "Love is a rose" is a metaphor because it demands that we imagine how love is like a rose. A metaphor can be understood as true only if taken **FIGURATIVELY**.

Our English word *metaphor* is borrowed from Greek. "*Meta*" means *trans-* or *across*, and "*phor*" means *port* or *carry*; thus, *metaphor* can be translated as *transport*. The metaphor above transports a *rose* from the world of gardening to explain something in the world of emotions, namely, *love*. Metaphors explain something in one world by transporting something from a distant world for comparison.

One way to analyze a metaphor is to sort its TENOR and VEHICLE, terms coined by I. A. Richards in his 1936 book *The Philosophy of Rhetoric*.

> ❧ The **TENOR** is the subject of the metaphor—what the speaker is talking about.

> ❧ The **VEHICLE** is what is transported for comparison to illuminate some quality of the tenor.

> In the metaphor "love is a rose," *love* is the tenor and *rose* is the vehicle.

The combination of a metaphor's vehicle and tenor prompts you to recognize that you're hearing or reading a metaphor because the statement would be otherwise absurd or impossible. As Richards emphasizes, the interaction of the tenor and the vehicle produces the metaphor's meaning.

Take, for example, the opening of Shakespeare's Sonnet 68:

> Thus is his cheek the map of days outworn,

When we read this line, we realize that a literal cheek cannot also be a literal map, and so we know that we're reading a metaphor. Here *cheek* is the tenor—what the speaker is talking about—and *map* is the vehicle—what the speaker has transported from the world of diagrams, paper, and ink to describe "cheek" by comparison.

Sometimes it is helpful to sort the metaphor's vehicle and tenor in a chart:

vehicle	:	tenor
map	:	cheek

And sometimes it is helpful to sketch the metaphor, trying to show both its vehicle (cheek) and its tenor (map). Here is an example:

G. Minette

☙ A **SIMILE** asserts that one thing is "like" or "as" another thing and demands that we imagine how.

"Lucinda is like her grandmother" is not a simile. It is a **LITERAL** statement.

"Lucinda is like a hurricane" is a simile. It is a **FIGURATIVE** statement.

Of course we may have to figure out how Lucinda is like her grandmother, but comparing Lucinda and her grandmother—who both are human, female, and kin—doesn't demand that we use our imagination to find similarities in altogether different categories of things as we must if we are to understand how a human being is like a storm.

Like metaphors, similes work by comparison, but with the word *like* or *as*, similes indicate their comparisons more explicitly. Similes announce the relationship between the tenor and vehicle more formally. After Egeus complains that his daughter Hermia will not consent to marry Demetrius, the duke, Theseus, instructs Hermia:

To you your father should be as a god, (1.1.47)

Here, when Theseus advises Hermia to obey her father or suffer the consequences, he transports *a god* to describe *father*. You could chart the simile:

vehicle	:	tenor
a god	:	father

The metaphor that opens Sonnet 68 articulates both tenor and vehicle—the cheek and the map—and makes clear their relationship: the cheek "is" the map. Sometimes, however, a metaphor does not name both tenor and vehicle. Or sometimes a metaphor does not state so clearly how the vehicle corresponds to the tenor. Such metaphors require more interpretation. Consider, for example, Helena's complaint about her beloved Demetrius's change of heart. (*Ere* means "before"; *eyne* is an alternate form of "eyes.")

> For ere Demetrius looked on Hermia's eyne,
> He hailed down oaths that he was only mine.   (1.1.242-3)

We know that Helena speaks a metaphor because Demetrius cannot have *hailed down oaths* literally. But Helena doesn't say explicitly what corresponds to Demetrius's having "hailed" them.

We can start interpreting the metaphor by charting:

vehicle	:	tenor
hailed down	:	?

Then, we can make a logical interpretation based on the context of Helena's statement and the nature of the vehicle, namely, *hail*. Often more than one interpretation is possible. For instance, we could say:

vehicle	:	tenor
hailed down	:	spoke (oaths) too numerous to count

Or we could say:

vehicle	:	tenor
hailed down	:	spoke (oaths) with great emphasis

Sometimes a statement or speech articulates more than one part of a metaphor's vehicle or tenor. Consider again, Helena's complaint, which continues:

> *Helena*　　For ere Demetrius looked on Hermia's eyne,
> 　　　He hailed down oaths that he was only mine.
> 　　　And when this hail some heat from Hermia felt,
> 　　　So he dissolved, and showers of oaths did melt.　　　(1.1.242-5)

Here are four steps that can help lead to an accurate and productive analysis of such a metaphor. I have included sample analysis for each step.

STEP 1. IDENTIFY THE METAPHOR'S SPEAKER, AUDIENCE, & CONTEXT.

Jot down speaker and audience, and briefly review the immediate and relevant context of the speech.

Example:

> Helena to Self or Audience. Hermia and Lysander have just told Helena that they plan to elope. Once alone, Helena laments how her beloved Demetrius, who once had loved her, now dotes on Hermia. Helena describes how Love is inconstant and lacks judgment.

STEP 2. IDENTIFY THE METAPHOR'S VEHICLES.

Underline all the elements of the metaphor's vehicle in the speech.

> *You can find a metaphor's vehicle by looking for the parts that would be absurd if taken literally with the tenor. Here you can recognize that "hail" is part of the vehicle because it would be absurd to imagine that Demetrius is a storm. Likewise, you can recognize that "dissolves" is part of the vehicle because Demetrius hasn't literally dissolved.*

Example:

> For ere Demetrius looked on Hermia's eyne,
> He <u>hailed down</u> oaths that he was only mine.
> And when this <u>hail</u> some <u>heat</u> from Hermia felt,
> So he <u>dissolved</u>, and <u>showers</u> of oaths did <u>melt</u>.

STEP 3. SORT THE METAPHOR'S VEHICLE & TENOR.

    A. Start by listing the elements of the vehicle and tenor the speaker states explicitly. Leave blank spaces for the corresponding parts of the vehicle and tenor implied.

Example:

vehicle	:	tenor
?	:	Demetrius/he
hailed down	:	?
hail	:	oaths
heat	:	?
?	:	Hermia/Hermia's eyne
?	:	he
dissolved	:	?
showers	:	?
melt	:	?

    B. Then, think about the analogies and fill in those blanks.

You might find it helpful to identify the worlds of the vehicle and the tenor. For instance, the vehicle here is from the world of weather and the tenor is from the world of relationships.

As you think about the analogies, be sure to review the full list of meanings of any key words.

As you identify missing parts of the vehicle, you might find it helpful to ask yourself questions like, "What literally would be hailed down in a storm?" or "What literally would cause showers of hail to melt?"

As you try to understand the tenor, you might find it helpful to ask yourself questions like: "What could affect Demetrius's oaths in the way that heat affects hail?"

Remember that filling in the blanks requires interpretation and that there may be more than one way to interpret accurately.

Example:

vehicle (world of weather)	:	tenor (world of relationships)
<u>storm</u>	:	Demetrius/he
<u>hailed down</u>	:	<u>spoke forcefully, passionately</u>
<u>hail</u>	:	oaths (of love for Helena)
<u>heat</u>	:	<u>desire (for Hermia)</u>
<u>the sun</u>	:	Hermia/Hermia's eyne
<u>the storm producing hail</u>	:	he (the man who made oaths to Helena)
<u>dissolved</u>	:	<u>was no longer (that man)</u>
showers (of hail)	:	<u>the speeches (of oaths)</u>
did melt	:	<u>no longer meant anything</u>

STEP 4. ARTICULATE THE METAPHOR'S MEANINGS & IMPLICATIONS.

First, think carefully about the metaphor's specific vehicle. In the case of this metaphor, think about the qualities of hail and storms. Then, think about how the qualities of the vehicle are transported onto the metaphor's tenor.

Keep in mind that not all of the implications and meanings of a metaphor are necessarily intended by the character who speaks the metaphor. Even if a metaphor's implications are not intended by a character, they nonetheless can acquire meaning in the play.

Example:

> Helena's metaphor compares Demetrius, who had spoken oaths of his love for her, to a storm that produces hail. Since hail occurs when there is a disturbance in the atmosphere, Helena's metaphor suggests that Demetrius's oaths of love were a product of some disturbance in him. Hail is forceful and can damage plants and hurt animals or people out in a storm; thus, the metaphor also suggests that a woman might need protection from a man's oaths of love, however exciting it might be to hear those oaths. Since storms end and hail eventually melts from its solid form to a liquid that seeps away, the metaphor further implies that oaths are likely not to last. Helena's metaphor suggests that a man's oaths can have a strong, harmful, and lasting impact even if the oaths themselves last only briefly.

Whereas metaphor and simile work by comparison, metonymy and synecdoche work by association or scale.

> 🕮 One thing standing for another associated thing is called **METONYMY**.

Puck uses metonymy when he petitions the audience, "Give me your hands, if we be friends" (5.1.425). *Hands* are associated with clapping, so "give me your hands" stands here for applause.

Puck also uses metonymy when he discovers the Athenian workers rehearsing their play and asks, "What hempen homespuns have we swaggering here" (3.1.64-5). *Hempen homespun* is a homemade, coarse cloth from which the workers' garments are made. Puck calls the men by the rustic, homemade clothes with which they are associated.

> 🕮 Part of a thing standing for the whole thing is called **SYNECDOCHE**.

Theseus speaks a synecdoche when he says, "The lover, all as frantic, / Sees Helen's beauty in a brow of Egypt" (5.1.10-11). A *brow* is part of a *face*, and a face is part of a woman. Theseus is saying that the lover sees Helen's beauty in the face of an Egyptian woman.

The difference between *being associated with* and *being part of* can be very slim, so it can be difficult to decide whether to classify a figure of speech as metonymy or synecdoche. The difference between metonymy and metaphor, however, is larger and more significant. In order to understand a metaphor or simile we need to imagine how a tenor in one world compares to a vehicle from a distant world: we need to imagine how one thing *is* or *is like* another thing with which it ordinarily is not associated. Unlike metaphor and simile, metonymy and synecdoche are from the same world as the things they stand for.

APPENDIX 3. ON HOW AN EDITION OF *A MIDSUMMER NIGHT'S DREAM* IS MADE

Anyone who publishes a Shakespeare play has made a number of decisions about how to transform the earliest surviving copies of the play into a current edition. As you develop your own interpretation of *A Midsummer Night's Dream*, it is helpful to be aware of what role an editor has played in making the edition of the play you are reading.

None of Shakespeare's handwritten play manuscripts has survived, and as far as anyone knows, Shakespeare was not involved in the publication of his plays. While Shakespeare was still alive, some of his individual plays were published in small books called *quartos*. A quarto of *A Midsummer Night's Dream* was published in 1600 (now called the *First Quarto* or *Q1*) and another in 1619, a reprint with minor changes (now called the *Second Quarto* or *Q2*). After Shakespeare's death, *A Midsummer Night's Dream* was included in a collection of Shakespeare's plays, entitled *Mr. William Shakespeares Comedies, Histories, & Tragedies*. This large book, called a *folio*, was first published in 1623. (Scholars now refer to this first edition of Shakespeare's collected plays as the *First Folio* or *F1*.)

Here is the beginning of Helena's first soliloquy as it appears in the surviving First Quarto and First Folio:

The 1600 Quarto

> *Hele.* How happie some, ore other some, can be!
> Through *Athens*, I am thought as faire as shee.

The 1623 Folio

> *Hele.* How happy some, ore other some can be?
> Through *Athens* I am thought as faire as she.

And here it is as printed in the 2005 Yale University Press edition of the play:

> *Helena*　How happy some o'er other some can be!
> 　Through Athens I am thought as fair as she. (1.1.226-7)

You will notice a number of differences between the early quartos and folio and any modern edition of *A Midsummer Night's Dream*:

- **Editors standardize spelling and punctuation according to current practices.** So, for instance, the First Quarto's "shee" is now printed as "she," and "faire" is printed as "fair." (You also will notice that "shee" is spelled with a "long s," a letter no longer available among English fonts.)

- **Editors add stage directions not in the Quartos or First Folio.** Often editors distinguish their own stage directions from those in the Quartos or First Folio by enclosing them in parentheses or brackets. During the performance of "Pyramus and Thisbe" in act 5, scene 1, after Bottom-as-Pyramus says, "Show me thy chink, to blink, through with mine eyne!" (5.1.176), the Yale edition prints the stage direction, "Snout stretches out his fingers." However, neither of the early quartos or the foilo includes a stage direction. Editors base such stage directions on their reading of the play, so you should always test them by reading the lines closely and considering other possible stagings. *(See question 14 on page 69 for an exercise on reading an editor's stage directions critically.)*

- **Editors mark act, scene, and line numbers.** The First and Second Quartos do not mark sections of the play with act, scene, or line numbers; the First Folio does not mark line numbers. Editors usually adopt the act and scene numbers marked in the First Folio, to which they add line numbers. Because some speeches in the play are in prose, not verse, a modern edition's line numbers vary depending on the size of the page. *(For explanations of verse and prose, see pages 73-4 of appendix 1.)*

- **Editors include notes that explain selected words and phrases.** In some notes editors provide definitions for words that might be unfamiliar to us now or whose meanings were different in Shakespeare's day. For instance, editors often note that the word *quaint* in "And the quaint mazes in the wanton green / For lack of tread are undistinguishable" (2.1.99-100) means *cunningly or ingeniously designed*—not *dainty*, as it might now, or that the word *blood* in Theseus's advice to Hermia, "examine well your blood" (1.1.68) means *emotions, feelings, or passions*. Editors do not list all possible definitions of words they gloss, but you can check the *Oxford English Dictionary* for a complete list of seventeenth-century meanings of any word. In other notes editors may offer more extensive explanations of the meaning of a phrase or a line. Read such notes critically: there may be additional ways to understand the phrase or line.

The choices editors make about what to include in an edition of *A Midsummer Night's Dream* depend on their theories about the sources of the early texts. Some basic information about each:

The 1600 Quarto. The title page of this earliest existing quarto reads: "A Midsommer nights dreame. As it hath been sundry times publickely acted, by the Right honourable, Lord Chamberlaine his seruants. Written by William Shakespeare." (The letters "u" and "v" were interchangeable in Shakespeare's day!) Although there is no way to know for sure, some scholars believe that the 1600 quarto may have been printed from Shakespeare's *foul papers*, a rough draft of the play that eventually would have been replaced by a *fair copy* provided to the players. Scholars who believe this theory note that this quarto's stage directions are not as complete as those in the 1623 Folio and that the speech headings for characters vary, for instance, from "Puck" to "Rob" (for Robin Goodfellow) and from "Titania" to "Que" (for Queen).

The 1619 Quarto. The title page of this second quarto copies the first except that it lists a different printer—Iames Roberts instead of Thomas Fisher. Although the date of publication noted is 1600, scholars have determined that this reprinting was, in fact, issued in 1619. The second quarto seems to correct certain printing errors in the first quarto, but it introduces others.

The 1623 Folio. Seven years after Shakespeare's death, two of his fellow actors, John Heminges and Henry Condell, collected and edited the thirty-six plays of the First Folio. The First Folio divides the play into five acts, and it adds or expands approximately thirty stage directions. Its title page advertises that it contains the plays "Published according to the True Originall Copies." None of Shakespeare's handwritten play manuscripts—no "true" or "original" copy—has survived. Moreover, as a playwright who was part-owner of a theater company, Shakespeare may have revised his plays during the course of their various performances or adapted them for particular occasions, further complicating the idea of an "original" or "perfect" copy. (*Perfect* can mean *complete*.) If, as most scholars believe, Shakespeare himself was not involved in the publication of his plays, then he did not make any choices about their publication.

Most modern editions of *A Midsummer Night's Dream* are derived largely from some combination of the 1600 Quarto and the 1623 Folio. Editors have to make choices when there are differences in the early texts. For instance, in the First Folio's act 5, scene 1, Theseus calls "Egeus" to ask about the evening's entertainment whereas in the first quarto Theseus calls "Philostrate" (5.1.38). Most modern editors follow Q1 in this case. You can compare your edition of *A Midsummer Night's Dream* to the early texts by finding facsimiles of them in your library or on the Internet.[2]

---

[2] Here are two websites that you might find particularly useful:
The Shakespeare Quarto Archives at http://www.quartos.org/index.html
Internet Shakespeare Editions at http://internetshakespeare.uvic.ca/Library/facsimile/

ACKNOWLEDGMENTS

Over the years I have had the pleasure of reading Shakespeare's plays with hundreds of students at Friends Seminary. Their enthusiastic interest in the plays, their willingness to work to understand them, and their fresh interpretations first inspired me to develop and publish guides to the plays. Exchanges with colleagues and students at other schools have encouraged me to continue the series.

Lauren Simkin Berke has once again designed the cover for the guide: I continue to be thankful for Lauren's imaginative reading and exceptional craft. I also continue to be grateful to Robert Lauder, Principal of Friends Seminary, for his gracious support and to my colleagues for their enduring camaraderie and help. Heather Cross convinced me to make the guides available to the general public, made key suggestions about their structure, and responded generously to many questions. Chris Doire, Josh Goren, Philip Kay, Cara Murray, Thomas O'Connell, Katherine Olson, and Craig Saslow offered valuable comments as I developed the guides' preface and appendices.

I am grateful to Donna Anstey at Yale University Press for permission to include an image of two lines scanned from the 1954 Yale University Press facsimile edition of *Mr. William Shakespeares Comedies, Histories, & Tragedies* and to Michael J. B. Allen for permission to include an image of two lines scanned from the University of California Press's 1981 facsimile edition, *Shakespeare's Plays in Quarto*, edited by Michael Allen and Kenneth Muir.

My understanding of—and delight in—*A Midsummer Night's Dream* is rooted in countless conversations with Sarah Spieldenner about teaching the play; I am thankful for our ongoing exchanges and for her excellent suggestions about this guide. I am grateful to Patrick Morrissey for his vital suggestions about the appendices, his discerning comments on the questions, and his careful editing of the manuscript. Final thanks are to Gordon Minette for help with matters large and small as I prepared *A Guide to Reading Shakespeare's A Midsummer Night's Dream* for publication.

www.ingramcontent.com/pod-product-compliance
Lightning Source LLC
Chambersburg PA
CBHW080446110426
42743CB00016B/3290